CAMBRIDGE
UNIVERSITY PRESS

CAMBRIDGE
Global English Starters

Learner's Book B

Kathryn Harper & Gabrielle Pritchard

Welcome!

Cambridge Global English is a ten-stage course for learners of English as a Second Language (ESL). The ten stages range from the beginning of primary (Starters–Stage 6) to the end of lower secondary (Stages 7–9). It is ideal for all international ESL learners, and particularly for those following the Cambridge Primary and Lower Secondary English as a Second Language Curriculum Frameworks, as it has been written to adhere to these frameworks.

In addition to Learner's Book B, *Cambridge Global English Starters Activity Book B* provides supplementary support and practice. *Cambridge Global English Starters Fun with Letters and Sounds B* offers intensive practice in reading and writing the upper- and lower-case letters learnt in lesson 4a of each unit. Comprehensive support for teachers is available in the *Cambridge Global English Starters Teacher's Resource*.

The following icons are used in this Learner's Book:

🎧 1   Audio track number reference

⬆️⬇️   Differentiation

🧍   Personalisation

💭   Critical thinking

For further explanation please refer to the teacher's resource.

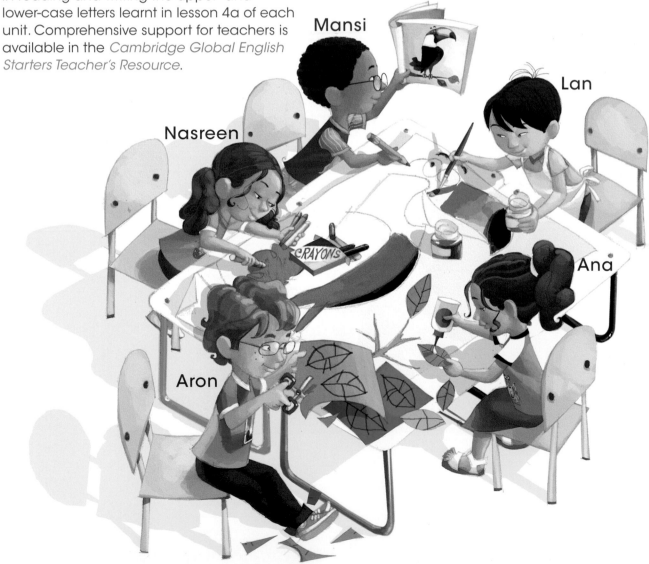

Mansi

Lan

Nasreen

Ana

Aron

Contents

Please see the teacher's resource for complete scope and sequence.

4 Play time!

🎧 1 ↕ Chant and clap.

A puzzle or game,
A balloon or ball,
A bike or kite,
There's fun for all.

2 💭 What can you see?
Explore the picture.

4 Unit 4 Lesson 1 Words: ball, balloon, bike, game, kite, puzzle Listen/Say: chant, sticking activity, game

3 ⬍ **Listen, say and stick.**

4 Play the game.

Can you remember the toys?
Pass the ball. Choose and say.

5

Our fun day

🎧 ³ 1 ↕ **Listen and follow the story.**
Look at the pictures. What are they playing with?

1

Look 👀 what I've got!

It's a purple balloon 🟣.
It's BIG!

2

Can you bounce it 🏀?

Yes. Look 👀! 1, 2, 3, 4.

3

I can fly a kite 🪁.
Can you?

Look out, Jake 😮!

4

Oh no! I can't
fly a kite 🪁.

It's OK.
Let's try something else.

Unit 4 Lesson 2 **Words:** purple/pink, bounce, fly, scared, ride, play **Listen/Read:** story **Speaking:** acting out story, talking about games, helping others

Unit 4 Lesson 2 Words: purple/pink, bounce, fly, scared, ride, play Listen/Read: story Speaking: acting out story, talking about games, helping others

2a What can they do?
Look at the story and match.

Rami can

Jake can

Amaya can

Jake can't

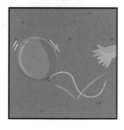

2b 💭 Who can play the game?
Tick ✓.

☐ ☐ ☐

3 💭 What can you do with a ball and a balloon?
Talk.

4 Act out the story.

5 Values
How can we help others?

3 Talk about it Playing – making and doing

1a Look at what we do for fun.

What do we play with? What do we make?

1b Draw lines to match to the correct box.

1c Ask and answer.

2 Play the colour game.

Give clues and guess.

It's red. What is it?

It's a red ball.

Unit 4 Lesson 3 Words: play/make, teddy bear, music, cake, climb a tree, tap knees, jump, bee, sing Language: Can you (make music)? Yes, I can. Listen/say: game, song

3a Look and tick ✓ the things **you** can do.

3b Listen, sing and act out.

Song: Can you climb a tree?

Can you play with me?
Can you climb a tree?
Yes, I can.
I can climb a tree.

Can you play with me?
Can you count to 3?
Yes, I can.
I can climb a tree.
I can count to 3.

Can you play with me?
Can you tap your knees?
Yes, I can.
I can climb a tree.
I can count to 3.
I can tap my knees.

Can you play with me?
Can you jump quickly?
Yes, I can.
I can climb a tree.
I can count to 3.
I can tap my knees.
I can jump quickly.

Can you play with me?
Can you buzz like a bee?
Yes, I can.
I can climb a tree.
I can count to 3.
I can tap my knees.
I can jump quickly.
I can buzz like a bee.

Can you play with me?
Can you sing loudly?
Yes, I can.
I can climb a tree.
I can count to 3.
I can tap my knees.
I can jump quickly.
I can buzz like a bee.
I can sing loudly!

5 **1a** Listen, point and say.

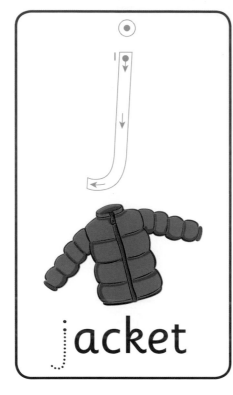
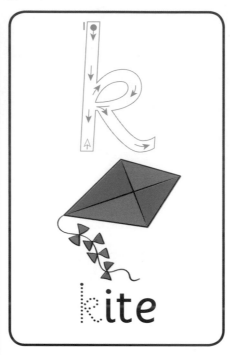

jacket

kite

leaf

6 **1b** Listen, find and trace.

7 **2a** Listen and say.

a b c d e f g h i j k l

2b 💬 Which pictures are missing?

Listen again. Then join and colour.

4b Let's learn our numbers

1 Look and say.

Write the numbers.

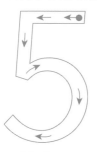

2a Listen and sing.

1, 2, 3,
I can see
3 big balloons
Flying up to the moon.

1, 2, 3,
4, 5, 6,
I can see
6 big balloons
Flying up to the moon.

Oh, no, no!
Now I can see
1 little bee
Flying up to the moon.

6, 5, 4,
3, 2, 1.
Oh, no, no!
The balloons are all gone.

2b Count and write.

5 Find out more Fun exercises

1a 🧍 Can **you** do these things?

1b Stick the **yes** 😊 or **no** 🙁 stickers.

Unit 4 Lesson 5 Words: kick, hop, jump Listen/say: doing actions, activities they like

2a Listen and do.

2b 💭 👤 Which activities do you like?

Reflection 💭

What makes an activity fun?

6 Our project

1a Make a game.

Work with friends. Think of a game that uses a ball 🎾 or a balloon 🎈.

Try out your ideas.

1b Show your game to the class.

2 Play the games.

Take turns to play the games.

3 Tell the class.

L👀k what I can do!

I can:

- 🙂 talk about how we have fun
- 🙂 understand a story
- 🙂 do PE activities
- 🙂 identify and say the letters and sounds **j**, **k**, **l**
- 🙂 count to 6

5 Let's eat!

1 Think about it — What do we eat?

🎧 10 1 ⬍ Chant and clap.

Spinach and carrots,
Peppers and onions,
Apples and mangoes,
What shall I grow?
I really don't know!

2 💬 What can you see?
Explore the picture.

3 ↕ **Listen and stick.**
Listen, say and act.

1 peppers

2 onions

3 carrots

4 mangoes

5 spinach

6 apples

4 ↕ **Go shopping.**
Play the game.

2 carrots, please.

Here you are.

Thank you.

The greedy goat

 1 ↕ **Listen and follow the story.**
Find the foods in the story.

1

I'm hungry.

I'm hungry.

I'm hungry.

2

Look **hot peppers** !
I don't like peppers .

I don't like **peppers** .

I like **peppers** .

3

1, 2, 3, 4, 5
hot peppers !

Yikes!

4

Look! Onions !
I don't like onions .

I don't like onions .

I like onions .

Unit 5 Lesson 2 **Words:** orange/brown, greedy, angry, goat, rabbit, duck **Listen/Read:** story **Speaking:** acting out story, food colours, food likes/dislikes, being greedy

2a What do Goat, Rabbit and Duck like?

I like peppers.

2b What are the food colours?
Look and match. Then colour.

orange

brown

green

red

2c 🗨 Some foods come in different colours.
Which ones are these?

3 Act out the story.

4 Values
Why is it bad to be greedy?

23

3 Talk about it   What do you like?

1a 👤 Complete the maze and talk about what **you** like and don't like.

> I like apples. I don't like peppers.

1b 💭 Look at your partner's maze and tell the class about it.

> Khalid likes potatoes.

1c 💭 Do a group survey about the mazes.

Unit 5 Lesson 3 Words: potatoes, nuts, lettuce, rubbish bin **Language:** I (like/don't like) potatoes. He/She (likes/doesn't like) potatoes. They (like/don't like) potatoes.
Listen/say: game, song

Stickers for Unit 4 page 5

Stickers for Unit 4 page 14

Stickers for Unit 5 page 19

Stickers for Unit 5 page 28

Stickers for Unit 6 page 33

Stickers for Unit 6 page 42

2a Listen and clap when you hear a food word.

 2b Listen, sing and act out.

Song: That greedy goat

Chorus:
Munch, munch, munch, munch,
Greedy goat's mouth's too full to sing.
Greedy goat likes everything!
Munch, munch, munch, munch.

That greedy, greedy, greedy goat,

Opens up his greedy throat,

Carrots 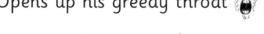, onions, apples in,

He is just a rubbish bin.

Greedy, greedy, greedy goat!

That greedy, greedy, greedy goat,

Opens up his greedy throat,

Mangoes, spinach, peppers in,

He is just a rubbish bin.

Greedy, greedy, greedy goat!

 1a Listen, point and say.

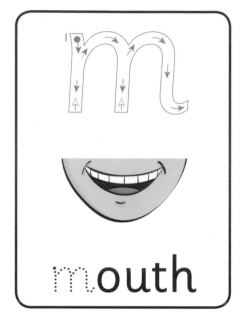

m.outh

nine

o.ctopus

 1b Listen, find and trace.

 2a Look at the picture.
Then listen, find and repeat.

 2b Listen again.
Trace the letters. Then circle the words.

mangonoseoctopusmouse

Unit 5 Lesson 4a Letters/sounds: m, n, o Words: mouth, nine, octopus Lesson 4b Numbers: 7, 8 Listen/speak: song Write: numbers 1–8

4b Let's learn our numbers

1 Look and say.

Write the numbers.

 2a Listen and sing.

1, 2  grow on a tree.

Out comes the ☀.

Now there are 1, 2, 3, 4 .

1, 2, 3, 4 grow on a tree.

Out comes the ☀.

Now there are 1, 2, 3, 4, 5, 6 .

1, 2, 3, 4, 5, 6 grow on a tree.

Out comes the ☀.

Now there are 1, 2, 3, 4, 5, 6, 7, 8 .

8 mangoes for you and me!

2b Count and write.

1a 💭 Are these things sweet or savoury?

What do you think?

 1b Listen and stick.

Unit 5 Lesson 5 Words: sweet, savoury, rice, bananas, ice cream, crisps **Listen/say:** discussing foods, trying foods, talking about foods they like

2a Make a food experiment with real or pretend foods.

2b Ask your friends to try your foods.

2c Make a food poster.

Reflection

What kind of tastes do you like?
Savoury? Sweet? Spicy? Fruity?

6 Our project

1 Make a poster puzzle.
Work with friends.

Choose an animal. Find out what it likes to eat.

2 Make your poster puzzle with friends.

Make animal and food pictures. Stick the pictures on your poster puzzle.

3 Can your friends solve the poster puzzle?

L👀k what I can do!

I can:

😊 talk about food

😊 follow and understand a story about a greedy goat

😊 talk about foods I like and don't like

😊 identify and say the letters and sounds **m**, **n**, **o**

😊 count to 8

😊 talk about sweet and savoury food

31

6 Let's listen!

1 Think about it What can we hear?

19 1 Chant and clap.

Clap quietly, clap loudly,
Tap fast, tap slowly,
Sing high, sing low,
Now, let's go, go, go!

2 What can you see?
Explore the picture.

Unit 6 Lesson 1 Words: fast, high, loud, low, quiet, slow Listen/Say: chant, sticker activity, game

3 ⇅ Listen, answer and stick.

Listen and clap.

loud
1

high
2

3
fast

4

5

quiet

6

slow

low

4 Play the music game.

Choose a leader. Take turns to conduct the class.

Sing high!

Clap fast!

2 Story time

The tiger and the woodpecker

🎧 21 **1** ⬍ **Listen and follow the story.**

What kind of noise does the bird make? Read, listen and find out.

1 I can run fast.

2 I can make a loud roar and jump.

3 Tap, tap, tap, tap, tap!

4 Quiet! Stop that tapping!

34   Unit 6 Lesson 2 **Words:** tiger, woodpecker **Listen/Read:** story, sounds **Speaking:** acting out story, saying story **Write:** trace words

Unit 6 Lesson 2 Words: tiger, woodpecker, sorry Listen/Read: story, sounds Speaking: acting out story, saying story Write: trace words

2 Trace what Tiger can do.

run   jump   roar   eat   fly   swim

3 💭 What does Tiger **not** like? Tick ✓.

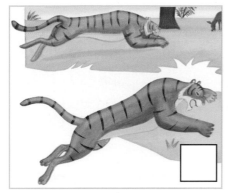

running and jumping

noisy birds

sticks in his mouth

rabbits

tapping

4 💭 Look at frame 9. Why does Tiger change his mind?

 5a 💭 Close your eyes and listen to the story.

Raise your hands high when it's noisy.
Put them down when it's quiet.

5b Make masks and act out the story.

6 Values
Why do we say 'sorry'?

37

3 Talk about it   What can you hear?

1 💬 Match the things to what you can and can't hear.

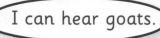
I can hear goats.

goat

teddy bear

can hear

carrot

drum

can't hear

guitar

bird

wind

tiger

sun

 2a 💬 **Listen and say what you can hear.**
Write the numbers.

 2b 💬 Is it loud or quiet?

 2c 💬 Is it fast or slow?   I can hear a drum. It's fast.

Unit 6 Lesson 3 Words: drum, guitar, piano, flute, wind, bird Language: What can you hear? I can hear (a drum). It's (fast) Listen/say: game, song

3a Listen and match.

 3b Listen, sing and act out.

Song: What can you hear?

Chorus:
Wiggle your ears.
What can you hear?
Wiggle your ears.
What can you hear?

Can you hear the drum?
Fast and slow.
Can you hear the flute?
High and then low.

Can you hear the guitar?
Fast and slow.
Can you hear the piano?
High and then low.

Now it's your turn.
What did you learn?
Can you sing
Just one little thing?

Go on ... sing!

1a Listen, point and say.

pencil

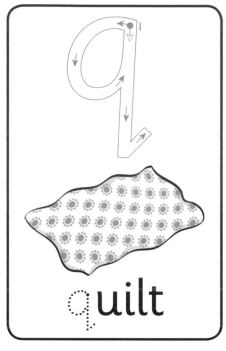

quilt

rain

1b Listen, find and trace.

2a Join and write the letter.

2b 💬 Can you find the sounds in the picture?
Listen and write the letter.

_acket   _ite   _eaf   _outh   _ine   _ctopus

4b Let's learn our numbers

1 Look and say.
Write the numbers.

 ## 2a Listen and sing.

1, 2, 3, 4.
4 big bubbles float up high,
4 big bubbles float on by.

5, 6, 7, 8.
8 big bubbles float up high,
8 big bubbles float on by.

8, 7, 6, 5.
5 big bubbles float up high,
5 big bubbles float on by.

4, 3, 2, 1.
1 big bubble floats up high,
1 big bubble floats on by.

2b Count and write.

5 Find out more How does music make us feel?

1a ⇅ **Look and say the feeling words.**
Add stickers for the new words.

happy ☐

sad ☐

excited ☐

scared ☐

relaxed ☐

like dancing ☐

 1b 💭 **Listen and describe each piece of music.**
Is it fast or slow? Is it loud or quiet? Can you hear any instruments?

 1c 💭 **How do the songs make you feel?**
Listen again and write numbers.

 1d 💭 **Listen again.**
Which songs are easy to clap to?
Why? Which song do you like best?

Unit 6 Lesson 5 **Words:** relaxed, excited, dancing **Listen/say:** discussing emotions and music, describing music

2a Listen.
Make movements to go with the music.

 2b Perform for the class.

3 🧍 **Think of a song that makes you happy.**
Sing it.

Reflection

When the music is fast 🐇, I feel …

When the music is slow 🐢, I feel …

6 Our project

1 Make an instrument.
Choose a drum or a shaker.

2a How to make a drum.
You need: a ▭, a small, coloured 🎈, an elastic ◯ and ◢.

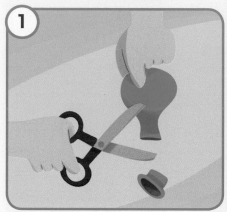

1

Cut.

2

Pull the 🎈 over the ▭.
Put the elastic ◯ over
the 🎈.

3

Stick ◥.

2b How to make a shaker.
You need: a 🍶, a ▭, different 〰, 🔖 and ◣.

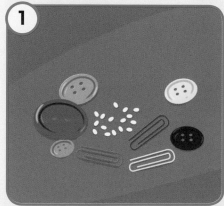

1

Choose and put in
the 🍶.

2

Cut the ▭ and ◢.

3

Stick ◣.

3a Experiment with your instruments.

3b Make music.

L👀k what I can do!

I can:

- 😊 understand what we can and can't hear
- 😊 follow and understand a story about a tiger and a woodpecker
- 😊 talk about things I can hear
- 😊 identify and say the letters and sounds **p**, **q**, **r**
- 😊 use the numbers 1 to 8

What can we remember?

 32 **1 Listen and draw lines.**

2 Count and write the numbers.
Then listen and check.

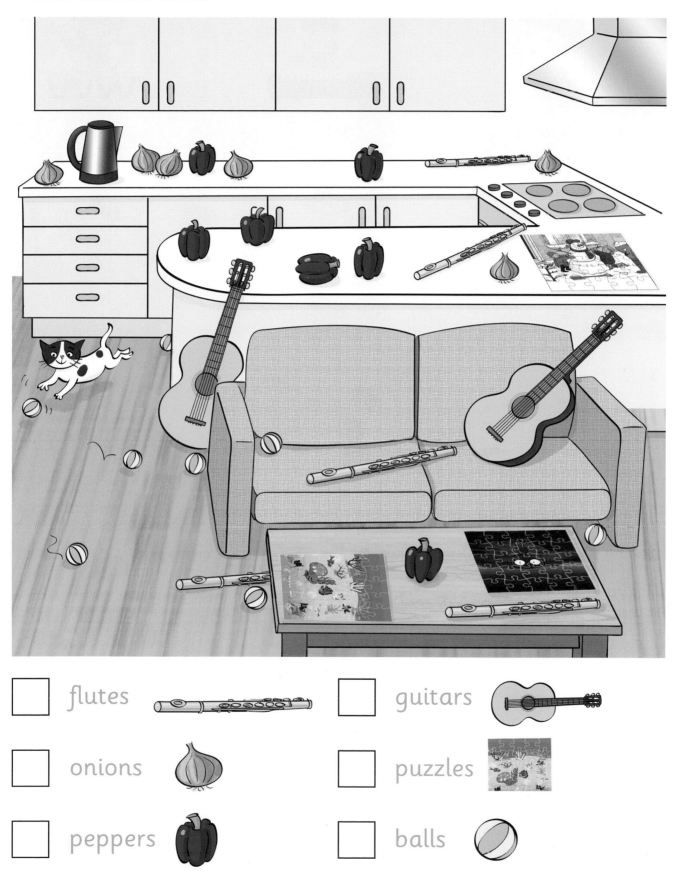

☐ flutes

☐ guitars

☐ onions

☐ puzzles

☐ peppers

☐ balls

47

3 Listen and tick ✓ the box.

1

a ☐

b ☐

c ☐

2

a ☐

b ☐

c ☐

3

a ☐

b ☐

c ☐

4

a ☐

b ☐

c ☐

5

a ☐

b ☐

c ☐